FOOTBALL LEGENDS

Terry Bradshaw

Jim Brown

Joe Montana

Joe Namath

Walter Payton

Jerry Rice

CHELSEA HOUSE PUBLISHERS

JERRY RICE

*Corinne J. Naden
and Rose Blue*

*Introduction by
Chuck Noll*

CHELSEA HOUSE PUBLISHERS

New York · Philadelphia

Produced by Daniel Bial and Associates
New York, New York.

Picture research by Alan Gottlieb
Cover illustration by Jon Weiman

5 7 9 8 6 4

Naden, Corinne J.
    Jerry Rice / Corinne J. Naden and Rose Blue.
       p.   cm. — (Football legends)
    Includes bibliographical references (p.   ) and index.
    ISBN 0-7910-2456-3 (hard)
    1. Rice, Jerry—Juvenile literature. 2. Football players-United
States—Biography—Juvenile literature. 3. San Francisco 49ers
(Football team)—Juvenile literature. [1. Rice, Jerry.
2. Football players. 3. Afro-Americans—Biography.]   I. Blue, Rose.
II. Title. III. Series.
GV939.R53N33 1994   94-4596
796.332'092—dc20   CIP
    [B]   AC

CONTENTS

A WINNING ATTITUDE

Chuck Noll

Don't ever fall into the trap of believing, "I could never do that. And I won't even try—I don't want to embarrass myself." After all, most top athletes had no idea what they could accomplish when they were young. A secret to the success of every star quarterback and sure-handed receiver is that they tried. If they had not tried, if they had not persevered, they would never have discovered how far they could go and how much they could achieve.

You can learn about trying hard and overcoming challenges by being a sports fan. Or you can take part in organized sports at any level, in any capacity. The student messenger at my high school is now president of a university. A reserve ballplayer who got very little playing time in high school now owns a very successful business. Both of them benefited by the lesson of perseverance that sports offers. The main point is that you don't have to be a Hall of Fame athlete to reap the benefits of participating in sports.

In math class, I learned that the whole is equal to the sum of its parts. But that is not always the case when you are dealing with people. Sports has taught me that the whole is either greater than or less than the sum of its parts, depending on how well the parts work together. And how the parts work together depends on how they really understand the concept of teamwork.

Most people believe that teamwork is a fifty-fifty proposition. But true teamwork is seldom, if ever, fifty-fifty. Teamwork is *whatever it takes to get the job done.* There is no time for the measurement of contributions, no time for anything but concentrating on your job.

One year, my Pittsburgh Steelers were playing the Houston Oilers in the Astrodome late in the season, with the division championship on the line. Our offensive line was hard hit by the flu, our starting quarterback was out with an injury, and we were having difficulty making a first down. There was tremendous pressure on our defense to perform well—and they rose to the occasion. If the players on the defensive unit had been measuring their contribution against the offense's contribution, they would have given up and gone home. Instead, with a "whatever it takes" attitude, they increased their level of concentration and performance, forced turnovers, and got the ball into field goal range for our offense. Thanks to our defense's winning attitude, we came away with a victory.

Believing in doing whatever it takes to get the job done is what separates a successful person from someone who is not as successful. Nobody can give you this winning outlook; you have to develop it. And I know from experience that it can be learned and developed on the playing field.

My favorite people on the football field have always been offensive linemen and defensive backs. I say this because it takes special people to perform well in jobs in which there is little public recognition when they are doing things right but are thrust into the spotlight as soon as they make a mistake. That is exactly what happens to a lineman whose man sacks the quarterback or a defensive back who lets his receiver catch a touchdown pass. They know the importance of being part of a group that believes in teamwork and does not point fingers at one another.

Sports can be a learning situation as much as it can be fun. And that's why I say, "Get involved. Participate."

CHUCK NOLL, the Pittsburgh Steelers head coach from 1969–1991, led his team to four Super Bowl victories—the most by any coach. Widely respected as an innovator on both offense and defense, Noll was inducted into the Pro Football Hall of Fame in 1993.

Dec
ecember 6, 1992. In San Francisco, California, it was a day for ducks, not outside sports. The 50 yardline in Candlestick Park, home field of the 49ers, looked as if it were in the middle of a monsoon. The field was waterlogged, and the players were drenched. More than 58,000 fans in raincoats huddled in the stands.

It was not a good day to play football.

Pro football players, however, are a rare breed. On this sloppy Sunday afternoon, the San Francisco 49ers were not as concerned about the weather as about the 11 players facing them across the line of scrimmage. The 49ers really needed to win this late-season game. A victory would give them an 11-2 record and keep them tied with the Dallas Cowboys in the race for home field advantage in the playoffs.

Winning would not be easy, for San Francisco's opponent on this soggy day was the

Jerry Rice celebrates after scoring his 100th receiving touchdown in the November 1992 game against the Philadelphia Eagles.

Miami Dolphins. The Dolphins were led by quarterback Dan Marino, one of the game's greatest passers, and Pro Bowl receivers Mark Clayton and Mark "Super" Duper. Their passing attack was rated number three in the National Football League (NFL), as opposed to the 49ers' pass defense, which was rated number 28—in other words, last in the NFL. Also, San Francisco was without its starting tailback, Roger Craig, who was injured. And the team's best offensive lineman would go down with a knee sprain early in the game.

Even so, it might be said that the 49ers had an unfair advantage. His name was Jerry Lee Rice. And he just may be the best wide receiver to play the game of football. Ever.

The San Francisco 49ers played inspired ball. Their defense held Marino and the Dolphins to 19 pass completions and 192 yards—far less than the Dolphins usually averaged. The Niners' offense was able to move the ball and, just as importantly, hold on to it. They turned the ball over only once in the game. And unlike the Dolphins' pass catchers, Jerry Rice hung on to the ball.

Still, Flash 80—Rice's nickname came from his deceptive speed and the number on his jersey—was frustrated for much of the game. In the second quarter, with a first down on the three yardline, Steve Young threw a quick swing pass to Flash 80, who stepped smartly across the left marker of the end zone. Touchdown! But was it? No, the official indicated that Rice had gone out of bounds before crossing the end zone; he marked the ball at the one yardline.

Near the end of the quarter, Rice got clear again deep downfield. Steve Young, the quarter-

back, rushed to get him the ball, but he under-threw it. The Dolphins intercepted.

In the third quarter, Rice sprinted clear in the end zone. Young saw him, but too late to get him the ball.

By the fourth quarter, Rice had 7 catches for 79 yards and no touchdowns. With 8 minutes and 56 seconds left in the game, Young called Rice's number in the huddle. Recalled Flash 80, "I said to myself that if Steve throws me the football, I'm just going to go up, make the catch, and take the hit. There's no way the defensive back is going to separate me from the ball."

And that's the way it happened. On a 12-yard pass from Young, Jerry Rice found an open

In the first quarter against the Miami Dolphins in a 1992 game, Jerry Rice was heading for the end zone— but Troy Vincent leaped and grabbed him in a last-ditch effort to prevent the touchdown.

spot in the end zone, arched his athlete's body gracefully in the air, and clutched the football in his right hand. Touchdown!

The score was 27-3. Miami's chances to come back from that deficit were nil. But the 49ers were happy for yet another reason. This catch was Jerry Rice's 101st touchdown reception. With it, he broke the record for most career touchdown receptions previously held by Steve Largent, the recently retired Seattle Seahawk. Largent had broken Don Hutson's record of 99 touchdowns, which the charter member of the Hall of Fame had set with the Green Bay Packers several decades before. It took Largent 200 games to catch 100 touchdown passes.

Rice had been chasing Largent's record for several years; now the pressure was over. Touchdown number 101 came in his 121st game, in his eighth career season in the pros, at age 30.

After the catch, Rice's teammates mobbed him in the end zone and carried him off the field. The crowd cheered even in the rain. Rice stood on a bench at the sideline and held the ball up so they could see it. Then he ran into the grandstand and hugged his wife, Jackie.

Guy McIntire, the 49er guard who witnessed all 101 catches, said afterwards, "This record, it's going to be tough to break, because he's nowhere near the end."

Don Shula has seen all the best receivers in his nearly three decades as an NFL head coach. He has watched such greats as Raymond Berry of the Baltimore Colts, Lance Alworth of the San Diego Chargers, "Bullet" Bob Hayes of the Dallas Cowboys, Fred Biletnikoff of the then Oakland Raiders, and the outstanding Steve Largent.

Said Shula after Rice's record-breaker, "He's in a class by himself."

Flash 80 broke other records that day in 1992. He became the ninth player in NFL history to go over 10,000 receiving yards in a career. He moved into ninth place on the NFL's all-time reception list. He took over sole possession of fifth place on the all-time NFL touchdown list. And he established a few 49ers team records as well.

The victory that day helped position the 49ers in the playoffs. Jerry Rice already owned two Super Bowl rings, but he wanted another— and another. Unfortunately for Rice, in 1992 Dallas defeated San Francisco and went on to win the Super Bowl.

Jerry Rice has had the good fortune to play on a team that had not one but two great quarterbacks—Joe Montana and Steve Young. The 49ers usually had excellent seasons, almost always going to the playoffs, winning several Super Bowls, and usually finishing high in the offensive statistic rankings. But Rice has often had to compete with his own teammates in order to get to catch the ball. The Niners were always willing to throw to their running backs: Roger Craig was the first back ever both to run for 1,000 yards and catch passes for 1,000 yards in one season. San Francisco always had at least one other top flight receiver on the field along with Jerry Rice.

None of the quarterbacks throwing to Steve Largent, on the other hand, were as good as either Montana or Young; and the Seahawks rarely won as many games as they lost. Still, Largent was often the only offensive threat that they had. He could count on numerous balls being thrown his way.

As any athlete knows, records are made to be broken. And Jerry Rice keeps on breaking them. This amazing athlete continues his climb to the top in every receiving category in pro football. Still playing at the top of his game, Flash 80 in action is a joy to see. When great athletes display their prodigious talents, they are sometimes compared to great ballet dancers. When they do it right, there is a near perfect harmony of art, strength, and talent—the powerful crack of the bat by Barry Bonds, the sky-high ride of a golf ball from Jack Nicklaus, the loud *whop* of a tennis ball placed just inside the line by Steffi Graf.

Jerry Rice is that kind of athlete. At 6′2″ and 200 pounds, he has the perfect receiver's body. His hands are large, his frame is long, lanky, and mostly legs. Other receivers are faster than Rice. Even he admits that his speed is only "moderate." But he has a knack for getting open, and once he catches the ball, he seems not to run but to glide down the field. His powerful legs churn into overdrive as he heads for the end zone. There's a beauty to his stride. The great ones possess unusual beauty.

But even the great ones aren't just born that way. They must take their raw talent and refine it with hard work and concentration. Jerry Rice, born in the backwaters of Mississippi and from a college few football fans have ever heard of, devoted himself fully to becoming the best player he could be. He succeeded.

R. C. Owens, former 49er end, once said of Jerry Rice: "He gets off the line. He has three speeds and changes them at any time. Of all the guys I've watched in now more than four decades, Jerry Rice epitomizes what the position is all about."

Wide receivers aren't supposed to be deciding factors in the game. Quarterbacks usually are, running backs are, occasionally linebackers. But Jerry Rice has worked so hard to develop his talents that former 49er coach Bill Walsh—in an act of extraordinary praise—once allowed that Rice was "the single most dominating player in the game today."

2

MISSISSIPPI RUNNING

Ask Jerry Rice what turned him into a star athlete, and he will probably tell you it was Mississippi running. "That's what made me," he told a reporter, "running those back dirt roads and country fields."

The dirt roads and country fields Rice referred to are back home in Crawford, Mississippi. Rice has taken lots of kidding about the size of his hometown in the northeast-central part of the state. He admits it's rural, but he smilingly says that Crawford, population 500, is a suburb of Starkville, the seat of Oktibbena County. (Actually, Crawford is 38 miles from Starkville.) Starkville is where you catch the bus to Jackson. Jackson is the capital of the state. And, as a *Sports Illustrated* writer once noted, "from Jackson, two or three plane rides will get you anywhere."

Jerry Rice wore number 88 all through college. Here he poses along with some of his teammates—including quarterback Willie Totten (number 10)—during the 1984 preseason.

Jerry Rice was born in Crawford on October 13, 1962. He is the fifth son of the six boys and two girls born to Joe B. and Eddie Rice. The Rice children soon learned that if you wanted to get anywhere in Crawford, you walked, or, in Jerry's case, you ran. He ran five miles to school in the morning and five miles home again in the afternoon, often after football practice. He and his brothers also ran after the horses that roamed the open pastures of the neighboring acres. If the boys wanted a horseback ride, they had to chase down the horses first.

Rice once described Crawford as a place that had "no sidewalks, no streetlights, no traffic, no sirens." It also had "no drugs and no crime." No one was wealthy in Crawford, and everyone knew and looked after everyone else.

Rice recalls a poor but happy childhood and a loving family. Although his parents had little in the way of material possessions, they provided their children with all that they could, especially support and caring.

During summer vacations, Jerry and his brothers helped their father, a brickmason, build homes in the county. The hard work helped mold him into a good pass receiver. He increased his upper body and muscle strength by pushing a wheelbarrow in the stifling summer heat. But most of all, he strengthened his large hands by catching bricks hour after hour.

Jerry remembers how he stood on a tall scaffold and got good at an unusual skill. "One of my brothers would stack about four bricks on top of each other and toss them up," he said. "They might go this way and that, and I would catch all four. I did it so many times, it was just a reaction."

His father said of Jerry that he "handled bricks better than any worker I ever had."

Besides catching bricks, Jerry also used his strong hands to fix almost anything that was broken—appliances, toys, furniture. He even thought about opening his own fix-it shop one day. However, those hands had a bigger future in store for him.

It was not until his second year in B. L. Moore High School that Jerry used his hands in his future occupation. It came about in an odd way. He cut classes one day, but was spotted in the school hall by the assistant principal. When Jerry heard his name called, he panicked and ran. Says Jerry, "All he saw was the back of my red jacket."

The assistant principal also saw a boy who could run. He told the football coach. Jerry was given the option of being punished for playing hooky or joining the football team. He chose football.

His mother wasn't happy. Eddie Rice was afraid he'd get hurt. Even with his brick work, Jerry was a slender young man who didn't look strong enough to take a pounding. "But," re-called Jerry's mother, "the more I fought it, the more determined he was."

Football wasn't the only sport Jerry tried. He also joined the track team and played for-ward on the basketball squad. With his speed, coordination, and grace, Rice was excellent at all the athletics he tried. But football was his clear favorite.

Jerry liked high school and his home town,

Jerry Rice set 18 records for Division I-AA receivers while at Mississippi Valley State University. Occasionally, he was allowed to throw an option pass as well.

but he was happy to leave when it was time for college. The world looks awfully big from Crawford, Mississippi—but the college he chose to attend was not all that different from where he used to live.

Mississippi Valley State University is located in Itta Bena in the western part of the state. About 2,000 students were enrolled there—more than the rest of the town's population. Itta Bena has a "city hall and the police station, and if you go another 100 yards, you're out of town," said Jerry.

Why did he choose to play for the Delta Devils? Because MVSU was the only college to send football scouts to look at Jerry play in high school. Jerry actually wanted to go to Mississippi State College, a much larger school that was only 21 miles away. But MSC wasn't interested.

Mississippi State was classified Division I-A by the National Collegiate Athletic Association (NCAA). Division I-A is generally where the best athletes play and where the pro scouts spend most of their time. Smaller Mississippi Valley State was classified Division I-AA.

Coach Archie "Gunslinger" Cooley used a standard pro-type running attack at MVSU— until he saw the lean young man from Crawford in action. Cooley knew he had found a dream wide receiver, and the green-and-white-clad Delta Devils became a pass-happy bunch. Cooley innovated a number of formations and a theory of football that has since become more widely played. Some of his ideas were inspired by basketball: his no-huddle, hurry-attack was the equivalent of fast-break basketball. He put four receivers on one side of the field, a look he got from basketball's inbound play. One of his unusual formations featured no running back.

Cooley wanted his quarterback to throw and throw. And he had an excellent quarterback in Willie "Satellite" Totten. Totten protested when Cooley asked him to eliminate the huddle and call all plays at the line of scrimmage. "The first

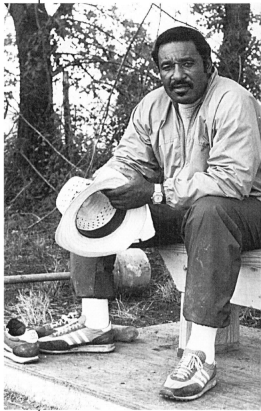

Coach Archie Cooley (with his trademark cowboy hat) created a new way of playing football so his team could take advantage of Jerry Rice's skills.

week with the no-huddle, I passed out, running up and down the field, it was so hot. A lot of guys passed out." The practices were so arduous, several of Cooley's defensive coaches protested.

"We'd score 15 or 20 touchdowns a day in practice," recalled Totten. "We thought, if we can do that to our teammates, who see it every day, what do you think we can do to a team which only has three days to practice for it?"

The result was an unprecedented form of football that was spectacularly successful. In their first game, MVSU defeated Kent State University by a score of 86-0. With Totten pitching the ball on nearly every offensive play, and with his roommate Jerry Rice catching every ball thrown his way, the Delta Devils were virtually unstoppable.

In 1984, MVSU gained an average of 640.1 yards per game. Passing accounted for 496.8 of these yards, as the team averaged 55.8 pass attempts per game. The Delta Devils scored an average of 60.9 points per game. All of these shattered previous NCAA records.

"It was so easy, it was amazing," Totten admits. "People would say if they walked to the restroom, when they'd come back we'd have two touchdowns."

In his four years at MVSU, Rice scored 50 touchdowns, 28 in his senior year alone, and chalked up 4,693 yards receiving the ball. He once caught 24 passes in one game. And although he was constantly double-teamed, he set 18 Division I-AA records.

The strong work ethic that his parents had instilled in him carried over to his college football days. When interviewed for this book, Willie "Satellite" Totten, now the football coach for the Delta Devils, said: "Jerry was the hardest working guy I ever saw in my life. He would go at full speed. I never saw anybody in such tiptop shape before. He would give you 100 percent on every play. It was amazing how gifted he was as a football player and receiver. He was naturally talented, but he never bragged about it."

Willie "Satellite" Totten, seen here with Jerry Rice, also set a slew of NCAA records. He was not chosen in the NFL draft; however, he did play pro ball in Canada and for the Buffalo Bills in the 1987 strike season.

Totten went on to say, "Off the field today, Jerry acts like a regular guy, not a celebrity. In college, he was fun, an all-around nice person. If you want someone to look up to, Jerry is the ideal guy. He's now a devoted husband and parent. He has his priorities in the right place. Other athletes have gotten into trouble because fame goes to their heads. I don't see that ever happening to Jerry. He's fast, he's meticulous, and he takes himself seriously as a role model."

Jerry Rice was a football star at MVSU, but one of his happiest days came when he attended a basketball game on campus with some friends. With them was a young woman who was visiting from Southern Mississippi University. Her name was Jackie Mitchell, and she immediately caught Rice's eye. Jackie had no idea who Jerry

Rice was or that he was already a campus hero.

Jackie remembers that the young man told her he would call the following day at noon. She figured that was the last she had seen of him. "The next day," she said, "he called right at twelve—on the dot." They soon became a couple, and all their friends knew they would get married. They were right.

Most college scouts had ignored Jerry Rice in high school, but few ignored him in college. How could they? Besides his regular season play, he was a consensus All-American and was chosen to play in the postseason Freedom Bowl All-Star Game and the Blue-Gray Game in his senior year.

Rice especially remembers the Blue-Gray Game. He was aware that getting drafted into the pros from tiny MVSU was not going to be easy. He had to show what he could do in the postseason games where the scouts could watch him matching up against top-notch competition. Most of the other players were from such football powerhouse conferences as the Big Ten. But Jerry was not intimidated. He regularly broke free downfield and caught two touchdowns. He was named the Most Valuable Player of the game.

Before the NFL draft each year, the *Current Biography Yearbook* offers information and tips on who the graduating seniors are. In 1984, the *Yearbook* reported that several pro scouts were doubtful that Rice could make it in the big league because "let's face it, the Delta Devils have played only mediocre opponents."

Coach Cooley had another explanation. "What they meant," he explained, "is that Jerry wasn't coached by a white man, so they had their doubts."

Willie Totten remembers the doubters. "A lot of the scouts weren't enthusiastic about him when he turned pro," Totten says. "But he sure proved them wrong."

3

JERRY *WHO?* AND THE ROOKIE BLUES

Many football experts thought Jerry Rice would not make it in the National Football League. But Bill Walsh wasn't one of them.

Walsh was hired as the 49er head coach and general manager for the 1979 season. Edward J. DeBartolo, Jr., owner of the club since 1977, was looking for a coach who could be a winner and create a closely knit organization. The 49ers had existed as a ball club since 1946 and as part of the NFL since 1950. But they had fallen on hard times. Before Walsh, San Francisco's last winning season was in 1976.

Walsh did not come up a winner until his third year, when the team rocketed to a 16-3 record and he was named Coach of the Year. Part of his success came from the passing arm of a young quarterback from Notre Dame named Joe Montana. "Golden Joe" and Jerry Rice were

The San Francisco 49ers put Jerry Rice through an arduous training camp when he arrived for his rookie season in 1985. But Rice has always kept himself in tiptop condition.

to become one of the league's most lethal passing combinations.

During his 49er coaching years, from 1979 through 1988, Walsh was highly respected by his peers. He engineered a complicated ball-control passing offense that had a strong influence on the way other teams would play during the 1980s. Under Walsh's direction, the 49ers chalked up 102 wins against 63 losses and 1 tie; their postseason game record was 10 wins and four losses.

Walsh had a special knack for uncovering raw, untrained football talent. He seemed able to spot a quality that others could not see. He spotted it in young Jerry Rice. Walsh had some doubts, naturally. He wasn't sure about the young man's speed or how he would stand up against the NFL's strong defenses. But the coach thought he saw a reliable deep-threat receiver, something his club lacked.

Walsh had experimented with other deep-threat guys, including Reynaldo Nehemiah, a world-champion hurdler. Nehemiah was probably the fastest man in football, but he had little football savvy and did not develop any consistency in catching the ball. After Nehemiah washed out, Walsh was no longer interested in pure speed. He wanted a complete package.

Walsh saw a potential complete package while watching sports highlights in a Houston, Texas, hotel room before a 49er-Oiler game. A

Bill Walsh was widely criticized when he traded away Steve DeBerg and named Joe Montana his starting quarterback. He was also widely criticized for choosing Jerry Rice in the first round of the 1985 draft. Fans, however, should always be grateful to him for creating probably the greatest quarterback-receiver combination in the history of football.

lean young receiver wearing number 88 began darting across the screen during the MVSU game highlights. There was 88 zipping in for a touchdown. There was 88 leaping into the air to bring down a pass thrown too high. There was 88 pulling down a ball with sure hands and leaving defenders behind in a dust cloud. "The hands, the body, the speed. What an absolutely majestic football player," thought Walsh.

Bill Walsh found out more about the flashy receiver in Itta Bena and decided that "if we didn't get him, some day we'd be playing against him." With that in mind, San Francisco's first choice in the first round of the 1985 NFL draft was from Mississippi Valley State, a school so small that there was no one else but the athletic director to write the press releases. Rice was the sixteenth player taken overall in the draft, the third wide receiver, and the first wide receiver ever picked as a first choice by Walsh.

Walsh figured he'd better be right on this one, because the 49ers gave up a lot for Rice. San Francisco went into the draft with the twenty-eighth pick as their first opportunity to claim a player. They traded that pick, plus one in the second, and another in the third round to the New England Patriots for the chance to pick sixteenth. It's a good thing they did. Walsh later learned that the Dallas Cowboys, which had the seventeenth pick, had been planning to take Jerry Rice.

Although Rice certainly believed in himself, even he was surprised to have been chosen in the first round. But imagine the shock at Mississippi Valley State University! Rice was the school's first first-round draft choice ever. It hasn't had one since.

The reaction of San Francisco 49er fans was shock of a different kind: Jerry *Who?* Few fans had heard of his school, let alone its star receiver.

"Once again, the 49ers blunder in their draft choice," pronounced one journalist in the *San Francisco Chronicle.* Even Walsh's scouts told him that Rice's talents deserved only a fifth- or sixth-round draft choice.

For a short time, it looked as though the fans, the sportswriters, and the scouts were right.

In 1985, Rice arrived in the 49er training camp driving a brand new BMW bearing the license plate WORLD. He explained that was what the students called him back at MVSU because he caught "everything in the world."

The statement sounded like bragging to the rest of the team. Veteran players always make rookies prove themselves, especially when they're highly touted and cocky. Rookies not only have to make the team, they have to earn the respect of their coaches and fellow players. Forty-niner teammates knocked him down on the practice field and played practical jokes on him in the locker room. Jerry Rice did play well enough in camp to assure himself a spot on the roster, but he did not excel enough to remove the questions people had about him.

Actually, Jerry Rice was going through culture shock. The young man from rural Mississippi had just arrived in the big city and was about to play in the big leagues. He was scared to death and trying not to show it. Also, he had signed a five-year contract for nearly $2 million with a bonus of $365,000. The boy who had grown up in hand-me-down clothes and worn-

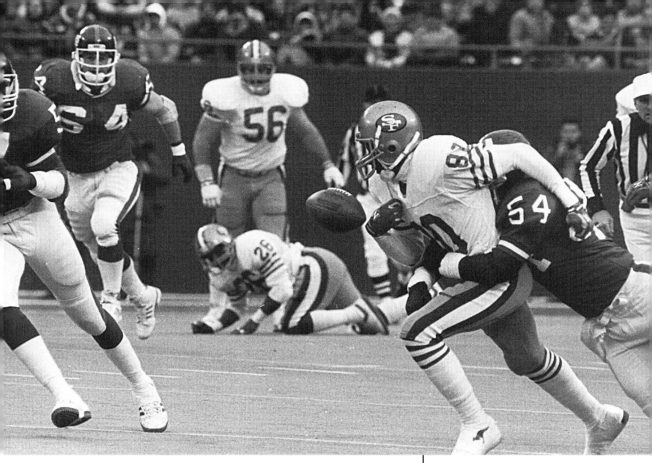

out sneakers now had more money than he had ever dreamed of. "I was out buying things all the time after practice," he said.

In college, the Delta Devils gave Rice a lot of freedom in the way he could create on the ball field. The 49ers, however, were much more strict. With the pros, he had to play by the book—the playbook. After he broke a pattern, his receivers coach, Paul Hackett, called him over to the sidelines and yelled, "You can't do that! You're not at Mississippi Valley State any more!" It took Rice an entire season to learn all the complicated plays the 49ers had in their playbook.

When Rice joined San Francisco, he was disappointed not to wear the number 88 he had

In his rookie year, Jerry Rice had trouble with fumbles and dropped balls. Here Andy Headen of the New York Giants strips Rice of a reception, and another Giant is about to claim the turnover.

worn in college. Veteran receiver Freddie Solomon wore number 88, and he had no desire to give the number up. So Rice took number 80—and he also took Solomon's starting job.

The fans were not pleased to see the popular Solomon demoted and the unknown Rice start off poorly. It took time for Rice to learn to adjust to Joe Montana's style of play. During this time, the usually surehanded Rice dropped an unusual number of passes. In a game against the Kansas City Chiefs, Rice dropped two catches in the first half. That gave him 11 muffs in his first 11 games. Many of his drops came when he was wide open.

The hometown crowd booed. Rice had never been booed before. At halftime, he cried. Some of his teammates tried to assure him that times would get better. Rice has admitted that he wanted to run off the field and hide.

That game was bad, but two weeks later, he had a worse day. In the game against the Washington Redskins, Rice did not catch one pass. He was frustrated, angry at himself, and scared of not measuring up. But he knew he had the talent and decided not to give in to negativity.

The following week featured a game between the 49ers and the Los Angeles Rams. Resolved to show his stuff, Rice caught 10 passes for 241 yards and 1 touchdown. He was the offensive star of the game. Flash 80 was on his way!

After a rocky start, Jerry Rice finished the season strongly. He caught 49 passes for 927 yards, an average of 18.9 yards per catch. That was the highest average in 49er history. Rice's statistics his first year were quite good, though nothing like some of the amazing years he yet would have. Nevertheless, United Press International and the NFL Players Association each voted Rice Rookie of the Year. The UPI vote was extremely close: he edged out Kevin Butler of the Chicago Bears by one vote.

The lean and lanky kid with the soft hands had his self-confidence back again. He knew he was going to make it big in the NFL. Bill Walsh knew it. Joe Montana knew it. And soon every football fan in the country knew it.

4

INTO THE
RECORD BOOKS

Weight makes a great wide receiver in the National Football League? Talent, strength, speed, good hands, quick reactions, and intelligence are all necessary. But what makes a truly outstanding wide receiver, one of the best ever to play the game? What makes a Jerry Rice?

Besides all the usual talents, no one really knows. There is just something extra. With his long and leggy frame, Rice seems to glide, not sprint, down the field. His speed is not so much blazing as elusive and tricky. Game after game, he is double- and sometimes triple-covered. Yet he consistently gets open. Up go those large hands, closing surely around the spiraling football. Another frustrated cornerback is left in the dust as Flash 80 heads for the goal line.

Dwayne Woodruff, cornerback for the Pittsburgh Steelers, once said that covering Rice was "like a horror show. He's so smooth when he's

Jerry Rice shows his elusivity by slipping past New Orleans Saints' Toi Cook. Rice scored a touchdown on the play.

running. He gets right on top of you and before you know it, he's by you. Once he is, I don't think anybody's going to catch him."

Rice himself feels that his speed is deceptive. His unusually long stride makes it appear that he is moving faster than he actually is. And he has an unusual ability to adjust to the ball at full speed after it has been thrown. Said Montana, "He just gets so open. He has the knack of knowing when to break, when to use his speed."

Says Rice, "I amaze myself sometimes."

Tim McKyer, a 49er cornerback, puts Rice's talents another way. "If you feed all the data of the ideal receiver into a computer, it spits out Jerry Rice."

Rice has great courage on the field as well. He is not afraid to risk his body by going after a pass while being hunted down by charging defenders. Yet he is rarely hurt and has never missed starting a pro game because of injury.

After his rookie year, Rice settled in at the 49ers' wide receiver spot and proceeded to put his statistics into the record books.

The 1986 season was a dazzler. In 16 regular season games, he caught 86 passes to lead the league. He gained 1,570 yards, the third highest single-season total in NFL history. He also scored 16 touchdowns. He was selected to the Pro Bowl and was named NFL Player of the Year by *Sports Illustrated*.

Rice especially remembers the game against the Indianapolis Colts. It put him on the right track, he says. In that game he had 6 catches for 172 yards and 3 touchdowns. The rookie blues were a thing of the past. In just his second season, Rice had become the most feared deep threat in football.

Contributing to Rice's success was the bond that he had formed with Joe Montana. The two started to click, and all the balls thrown by Montana's strong, accurate arm to Rice's soft, sure hands seemed guaranteed to help move the team downfield. Their success looked easy, but it was really due, said Rice, to "a lot of hard work during camps." That was when he got to know how Montana worked and how he should react in different situations.

The same was true for Montana, who said, "Jerry has the ability to go after the football. When you're in trouble, he's going to come running. So you say to yourself that he's around here somewhere. He'll find a way to get open."

As good a season as Rice had in 1986, it ended poorly for him. In the first quarter of a playoff game against the New York Giants, Rice got past the defense, caught a Montana pass, and took off running. There was no defender between him and the goal line. Startlingly, the ball fell out of his hands without a Giant touching him. One of the Giants chasing after him fell on the fumble.

Joe Montana high-fives Jerry Rice after he caught a 78-yard touchdown pass with 42 seconds left to win a game against the New York Giants.

The Giants won the game 49-3, so the lost touchdown didn't matter, although no one knew that at the time of the play. The Giants went on to win the Super Bowl, and Jerry Rice went home to brood about the freak play.

Even if the season ended sadly for Rice, it also silenced the critics and the fans and turned them into supporters.

The 1987 season was shortened to 12 games by a players' strike. Rice shattered two NFL records that should keep his name around for

Roland James of the New England Patriots knocks Jerry Rice out of bounds, but not before Rice sticks the ball over the goal line and inside the out-of-bounds marker. That's a touchdown!

some time to come. Rice caught 22 touchdown passes, breaking the record set by the Miami Dolphins' Mark Clayton, who had 18 in 15 games in 1984. Rice also caught touchdown passes in 11 consecutive games, breaking a long-time record shared by Elroy "Crazylegs" Hirsch and Buddy Dial. By the end of the year, he had grabbed TD passes in 13 straight games.

All during the 1988 season, Rice was bothered by an ankle injury. It reduced his receptions to only 64 in 16 games. Yet he scored three touchdowns in the divisional playoff game with the Minnesota Vikings on January 1, 1989. A week later, San Francisco faced the rough and tough Chicago Bears for the National Conference title. The game was played on the Bears' home turf in frigid midwestern winter weather. Although the 49ers were not used to such conditions, Rice predicted he would have a big game. "I'm healthy," he said, "and that's the difference."

It was. Rice gathered in 5 catches for 133 yards and 2 touchdowns, including one that went for 61 yards. That helped his team to an impressive 28-3 romp and headed them for Super Bowl XXIII.

The 49ers had already won two Super Bowls in the few years before Jerry Rice joined the team. On January 24, 1982, in Super Bowl XVI, Joe Montana played an inspired game to lead the Niners to a last minute victory over the Cincinnati Bengals, 26-21, in the Pontiac, Michigan, Silverdome. Three years later, on January 20, 1985, in Super Bowl XIX, they smothered the Miami Dolphins, 38-16, in Stanford, California.

Now Jerry Rice was going to play in his first Super Bowl. Most of the big names on his team already had won two championships. He hoped that his excitement at being in the big game was going to help keep everyone else on the team excited.

5

SUPER TIME

Ever since Jerry Rice joined the 49ers, he wanted to wear a certain type of ring. Rice was a flashy dresser and had already bought a diamond earring. But earrings can be bought with money. The type of ring Rice wanted could only be earned by a lot of hard work and great team play. He wanted a Super Bowl ring.

Of the tens of thousands of athletes who play college football, only a small percentage go on to play professional football. Of those who do get pro contracts, only a small percentage get to play in the Super Bowl. Every January, the top team from the American Football Conference faces off against the top team from the National Football Conference to see which team is the best in the world. Losers of the Super Bowl get a ring as well as the winners—but the winners' rings are bigger.

On the road to the Super Bowl, a team must win its division or gain a "wild card" spot by hav-

Jerry Rice leaps for a catch against the Cincinnati Bengals in the 1989 Super Bowl.

ing the top record of those non-division-winning teams. The playoffs pit these best teams against each other; the losing team goes home for the winter, while the winning team moves on to the next level of competition. It all ends with the showdown between the last two teams standing.

The Super Bowl only dates back to 1967—before then, the NFL season ended with a playoff game between the winners of the East and West divisions—but it has quickly become the most popular one-day sporting event in America. Millions of people watch the game on television, and businesses spend millions of dollars so that that audience will watch their advertisements.

Every pro football player dreams of being on a Super Bowl team. There are a lot of reasons why. Playing in the Super Bowl pays participants thousands of dollars in addition to their regular salaries. (Thirty years ago, when athletes received a lot less than they are paid now, the extra playoff money could mean a lot to the players. Jerry Rice, however, makes about three million dollars a year, and the extra money from a Super Bowl makes little difference to his lifestyle.) Another reward is that athletes who have starred in the Super Bowl can receive extra opportunities to make money on the side by making "personal appearances" or endorsing sports equipment or other products.

But most importantly, a Super Bowl ring means pride and prestige. Athletes never know when their last game will be, or when they will cease to compete at the level they've been used to. But an achievement such as playing in the Super Bowl is something that can never be taken away.

Super Bowl XXIII was a dream game for Rice. National Conference champion San Francisco, with a 10-6 season record, faced the American Conference leaders, the Cincinnati Bengals, who had gone 12-4. The game was played before 75,000 fans in the stands of Joe Robbie Stadium, in Miami, Florida.

The 49ers had started off poorly that year. In their first 11 games, they won only six and lost five. But San Francisco regrouped and went on a four-game winning streak that carried them into the playoffs.

For the first time in Super Bowl history, the game was tied at halftime. Each team had

The Niners show a little razzle-dazzle as Jerry Rice carries the ball on a reverse in the first quarter of Super Bowl XXIII. Joe Montana (#16) handed the ball off to Roger Craig (#33), who handed it off to Rice. Montana stayed around to throw a lead block for Rice.

Jerry Rice and Joe Montana go over their notes before Super Bowl XXIV in 1990.

scored a field goal to knot the score at 3-3. In the third quarter, another field goal apiece left the score tied again. Then, with just 34 seconds remaining in the quarter, the Bengals' Stanford Jennings returned a kickoff 93 yards to make the score 13-6. It was time for Joe Montana to get busy.

In four plays, San Francisco covered 85 yards. The big strike was a 14-yard scoring pass to Flash 80 just 57 seconds into the final quarter.

The 49ers' offense was clearly moving the ball more successfully than the Bengal offense. Late in the game, the Niners had amassed 453 yards offensively as opposed to 229 yards for Cincinnati. But the score was still tied at 13. With only 3:20 remaining, the Bengals' Jim

Breech kicked a 40-yard field goal, and that margin looked like it might be the difference in the game.

The 49ers took the ball on their own eight yardline. This was their last chance, they knew. And they were a long way away from the opponents' end zone.

Montana, in an amazing vision of calm and leadership, directed a masterful drive. He threw short passes to Roger Craig and one to tight end John Frank. Craig made two short runs to bring up a third and long at San Francisco's 35 yardline with under two minutes to play.

Jerry Rice broke free on the left sideline and Montana hit him for a 17-yard gain and a first down. Another pass to Craig brought another 13 yards and a first down. The crowd was going wild.

An incomplete pass followed, and a holding penalty backed the Niners up to the Cincinnati 45. On the next play, Montana could not find anyone open, so he threw to Jerry Rice hoping Rice could make something happen.

Rice was in the middle of the field, covered tightly by Pro Bowl cornerback Lewis Billups and safety Ray Horton. Still, he snagged the ball and evaded the Bengal defenders. He could not be tackled until he reached the 18 yardline. Two plays later, Montana hit wide receiver John Taylor in the end zone, and it was all over. San Francisco had won Super Bowl XXIII, 20-16.

The throw-and-catch show by Montana and Rice on just that day made fans realize what a Hall-of-Fame performance they had just seen. Montana completed 23 of 36 passes for 2 touchdowns and a Super Bowl record of 357 yards. Even that spectacular display was outdone by

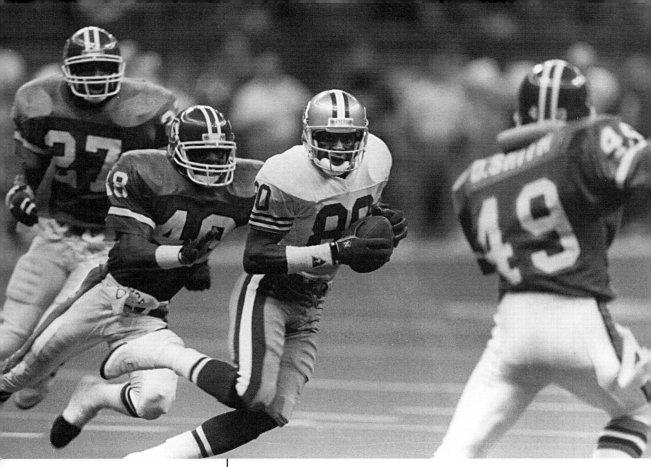

Jerry Rice was run down from behind by Denver safety Randy Robbins on this play. But in this 1990 game, he set a Super Bowl record by catching three touchdown passes.

Rice. He won the Most Valuable Player Award for his 11 receptions, 1 touchdown, and Super Bowl record of 215 yards.

After the Super Bowl, Denis Collins of the *Washington Post* said Rice was "the best receiver in football."

The warm glow of the win was tarnished a few months later when Rice made a controversial remark to the media. He complained about not getting the endorsements and commercial benefits that white players enjoyed. Joe Montana received offers to appear in numerous commercials; indeed, he even married an actress whom he met on one of the sets.

It has largely been true that black athletes have not had the same endorsement opportunities as white athletes, although recently the phenomenal successes of Michael Jordan and Shaquille O'Neal have changed the way many advertisers think. Nevertheless, fans and teammates were angry with Rice for his comment. Joe Montana was an extremely popular man all across America, while Jerry Rice was still young and not well known. They felt it was inappropriate to compare himself to a teammate and already certifiable legend. Rice later stated that he had been thoughtless and apologized.

Bill Walsh retired after Super Bowl XXIII, but new coach George Seifert carried on San Francisco's winning ways. Rice and the 49ers went to the Super Bowl again in 1990. With the help of Rice, Montana, and other veterans, the 49ers dominated their opposition and posted a 14-2 season.

In the playoffs, the Niners beat the Minnesota Vikings 41-13 and the Los Angeles Rams, 30-3. Rice scored twice in the Minnesota game, once on a 72-yard pass play. That victory earned them a spot against the Denver Broncos in Super Bowl XXIV.

A crowd of nearly 73,000 filed into the Louisiana Superdome in New Orleans on January 28, 1990, to see the contest between football's two top quarterbacks: Joe Montana and John Elway of the Broncos. Elway could throw the ball as far and hard as any human, and if he couldn't find a receiver, he could run with the ball effectively as well. The Broncos had posted an 11-5 record, and many sportscasters had expected the game to be tight.

It wasn't. By halftime, the 49ers held a 27-3 lead. They scored on four of their six possessions in the first half. The Broncos could not get

Rice had a lot to celebrate—as did his teammates—as they utterly devastated the Denver Broncos in Super Bowl XXIV.

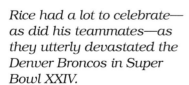

on track. Their first two possessions of the third quarter ended in interceptions.

The game turned out to be the most lopsided Super Bowl in history. San Francisco won, 55-10. Their 55 points broke the Chicago Bears' scoring mark of 46 points in Super Bowl XX. For the third time—a record—Montana was named Most Valuable Player for his efforts. He completed 22 of 29 passes for 297 yards. He threw for five touchdowns, which broke the record of four previously held by Terry Bradshaw of the Pittsburgh Steelers in Super Bowl XIII and Doug Williams of the Washington Redskins in Super Bowl XXII.

Rice caught three of those TD passes—also a record. In all, he caught 7 passes for 148 yards. Now he had a Super Bowl ring for each hand.

6

BEHIND THE NUMBER

Lots of kids dream of being rich and famous. But getting there can have a downside. For Jerry Rice, the downside at first was culture shock and a loss of privacy. Essentially a shy man, as a rookie he found it difficult to adjust to life in the big time and the big city. He was a naive and somewhat awkward country lad from Mississippi. When confronted with an army of clicking cameras and microphones, he retreated into a shell. He had no idea of what to say or how to say it.

But all that is in the past now. Rice went to a speech coach and learned how to be well spoken and poised in front of cameras and large numbers of people. Polished and well dressed, he now enjoys being in the public eye. He believes that athletes should be role models for young people in the way they act. And so, Rice tries to keep "his head on straight." He learned an ethic of hard work from his parents, and he brings

On the field, Jerry Rice is all business. Off the field, he likes spending time with his family and having fun.

that to every game he plays, and every day away from the field as well.

Rice is still close with his parents. Even with all his success today, if he has a bad game and feels he hasn't played well, he is apt to call his folks and talk about it. Rice, his wife, and children still spend part of the off-season back in Mississippi. After he became a pro, he built a home for his parents in Starkville. That, he says, gave him one of his greatest thrills.

Rice is also extremely close with his wife and children. Jerry and Jackie have two children, Jaqui Bonet, born in 1987, and Jerry, Jr., born in 1991. At one time Rice rented an apartment during the football season, but now the family is permanently established in a house in the San Carlos hills, not far from San Francisco. The household also includes two huge dogs, Rottweilers Max and Missie. Rice enjoys the lifestyle of the San Francisco Bay area. For relaxation, he likes to listen to soul music and go dancing with Jackie.

He also likes to maintain a neat image. Rice is a bug on neatness. Says Jackie, "Sometimes he comes home from work and instead of relaxing, he starts cleaning and straightening things up. I tell him to sit down."

Rice is also a bug on dressing neatly. That includes on the football field. You may see other players with their shirttails hanging out of their football pants or their socks slipped down around their ankles. Not Jerry Rice. After every play, he tugs at his socks, or adjusts his shirttail.

If a game starts at four o'clock, Rice is at the stadium at two to get dressed. His shoes have to be white, his socks have to be the right length, his helmet has to be clean.

"Some of the guys come in and just sit back and watch me get ready for the game," he says. "They can't believe I'm taking so much time with my uniform. But if I'm going to play sharp, then I'm going to look sharp."

By now, his teammates are used to Flash 80 and his style. In 1987, he showed up in training camp five inches taller than his usual 6′2″. The extra five inches came from his hair. It was cut very short on the sides and grew straight up from the top. His teammates took one look and began to call him "Fifi." They thought he looked like a French poodle. One 49er suggested sticking a tee on Rice's head and hitting golf balls.

Jerry Rice and wife Jackie are feted in a victory parade down San Francisco's Market Street after Super Bowl XXIII.

"Everybody had something to say about my hair," Rice recalls. "But you have to do something to have fun in training camp."

With his salary worth nearly $3 million a year, plus his outside endorsement income, and his investments, Rice should be comfortably off for the rest of his life. He has traded in his BMW for a flashier Porsche 944 and a Jaguar XJ6. But he knows money is not the most important element of the success he has reached. Being a good father to his children and a leader in his community are his top priorities.

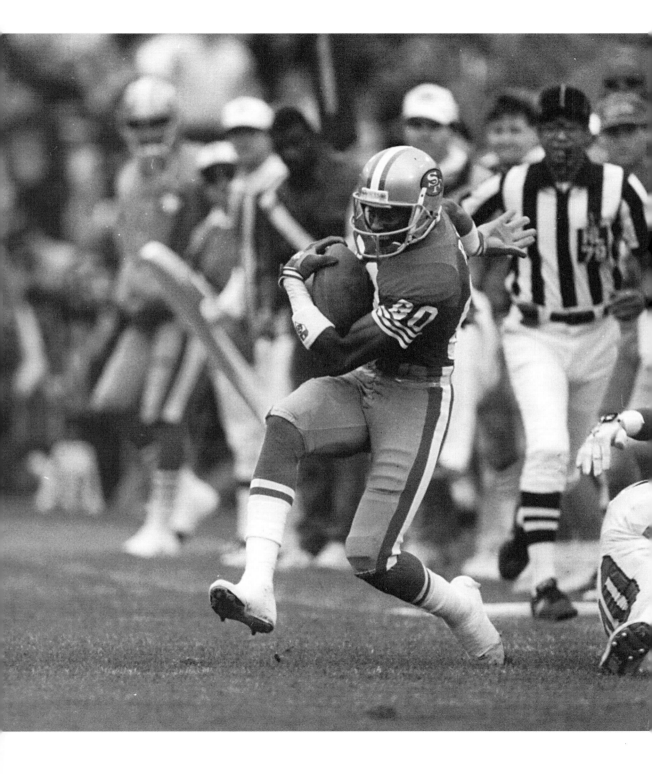

7

IT DOESN'T GET MUCH BETTER THAN THIS

Barring injury, San Francisco wide receiver Jerry Rice may break every record in the books for his position. "Zoom, zoom, and it's all over," said cornerback great Willie Brown. "That's what fooled people about Rice coming into the pros. They didn't understand his speed. They went by the stopwatch, but he had competitive speed, football speed."

Every year since 1986, Rice has led his team in several offensive statistics, or set a playoff record, or led the league in a key category, or established a new NFL record—or, most commonly, some combinations of these. In 1987, he led the NFL by scoring 138 points. In 1990, he became the 49ers' leading yardage gainer. In 1992, he became San Francisco's leading pass-catcher, and had set a team record of 106 consecutive games with at least one pass caught (a record he has since extended). He also became

Jerry Rice has made a career of leaving defensive backs in a heap on the ground as he tiptoes in for a touchdown.

the NFL recordholder for most postseason receptions and touchdowns. In every year since his first in the league, he has gained over 1,000 yards.

Jerry Rice has been averaging 84 receiving yards per game, far above the average of anyone else. Just to compare, Steve Largent's average was 65 receiving yards per game. Usually once a season, and sometimes twice, Jerry Rice outscores the opposing team all by himself. No one keeps official records on this—but here is another case where Rice is clearly in a class by himself.

At the beginning of the 1994 season, Rice was 32 years old and perhaps past the prime of his spectacular career. But he was still ready to be a major contributor on a 49er team where he had been a fixture ever since being drafted in 1985. Never seriously injured, he brought game-breaking talent to the line on every play.

Defensive backs have three ways of trying to stop Jerry Rice. First, they can try to stop him cold by playing him close and bumping him at the line of scrimmage. But Rice is so strong and fast he can make the backs miss their block, or escape it in seconds. Once he's past them, he's en route to a big play. Second, defensive backs can try to line up a few yards away from him and try to stay within two or three yards while Rice runs his pattern. But Rice has a great range of moves and fakes; even if a defensive back can keep up with him, Rice is still likely to catch the ball, put another move on the defender, and rumble on for a large gain. The third option is the least popular. Defensive backs can give Rice a lot of room to run, and key on tack-

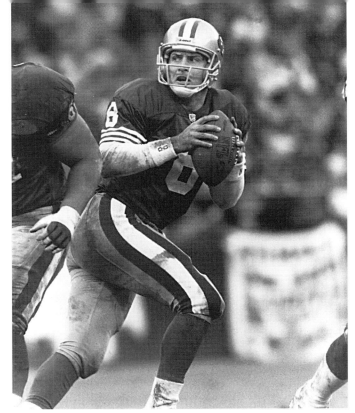

Steve Young plays a brawny, tough game of football, as opposed to the deft control that marks Joe Montana's style of play. Jerry Rice has been happy catching passes from either quarterback.

ling him once he gets the ball. In most cases, Rice will then settle for a modest gain on the play—perhaps seven or 10 yards. But that's considered a fine average per play; no team can win by letting the opponent do that all day long.

The only other defensive options are to assign two or three players to cover Rice—which usually means one or two other 49ers will be open—or try to intimidate Rice by tackling him hard and getting in his face. But usually the people who come away intimidated are the defensive backs.

Whether it's snaring a key catch, or making a downfield block, Rice is determined to find ways to help his team win. He is especially determined if the team is struggling.

Paul Warfield, the legendary receiver for the Miami Dolphins, said that Jerry Rice didn't get

Jerry Rice keeps on jogging towards the Pro Football Hall of Fame in Canton, Ohio.

the credit he deserved as a "great blocker for the running game." Rice admits, "I've really worked on that part of my game," he says. "I want to become a leader of the team."

Perhaps the biggest adjustment Rice has had to make since becoming an established pro football player is one he has not talked about much. Rice started his career as a favorite target of quarterback Joe Montana. But in the late 1980s and early 1990s, Montana was often injured, and Steve Young was the usual substitute. (Sometimes Young was injured too, and then the 49ers had to go with a third-string or even fourth-string quarterback.) At the end of 1992, Joe Montana came off the injured list, and was able to make a claim for a return of his starting status.

In the interim, though, Steve Young had made an excellent claim for keeping the starting status he had gotten used to. In 1992, while Montana was healing, Steve Young was named the NFL's Most Valuable Player. After a lot of hard thinking about the future of the team, the 49ers eventually decided to trade away the greatest quarterback in their history: Joe Montana.

The difference in styles between the two quarterbacks was great. Montana throws righthanded and prefers to drop back in the pocket, where he can stay protected by his linemen as long as possible before he releases his pass. Young throws lefthanded and is an excellent scrambler. If Jerry Rice was bothered by the quarterback controversy, or the difference in the styles of either player, he never showed it. Instead, he just kept grabbing every ball thrown his way, whether it was from Montana, Young, or any of their backups.

At the beginning of the 1994 season, Rice had 47 TD receptions from Young as opposed to 55 from his years with Montana at quarterback. In the fourth game of 1993, against the Tampa Bay Buccaneers, Young and Rice combined on *four* touchdown passes.

Steve Young once said of Rice, "I think he believes that if they covered him with 11 guys, he should still be open and win the game."

While Jerry Rice won't be eligible to join the Hall of Fame until after he retires, everyone expects he will be a shoo-in. Until then, he can take pride in having been named to the Sheridan Black Network All-Time Black College Football Team.

Dallas Cowboy star receiver Michael Irvin made the ultimate comparison. "They call Michael Jordan Jesus in tennis shoes," Irvin said. "Jerry Rice is Jesus in cleats."

Despite all the accolades, Rice keeps a level head. "It's not for me to say I'm the best."

What does Jerry Rice want to accomplish in his football future?

"When I finish playing, after 14 seasons or so," he said a few years ago, "I want people to say 'Jerry Rice was the best ever to play this game.' I know there are some very good receivers now—'living legends' like Steve Largent, for instance. But I think I can be the best ever."

There are many people who feel he's proved that already.

JERRY RICE:
A CHRONOLOGY

1962   Jerry Rice born in Crawford, Mississippi

1980   Enrolls at Mississippi Valley State University where he teams with Willie "Satellite" Totten and leads the most explosive offense in the history of college football.

1984   Finishes college career as a consensus All-American; named Most Valuable Player of the Blue-Gray Game

1985   Drafted in the first round by San Francisco 49ers, is named Rookie of the Year by UPI and NFL Players Association

1986   Leads NFL in yardage and receiving touchdowns, leads NFC in receptions; named NFL Player of the Year by *Sports Illustrated*

1987   Sets NFL records for most receiving touchdowns in one year and most consecutive games catching a touchdown; leads NFL in points scored; named 49ers' Len Eshmont Award for most courageous player; named NFL Most Valuable Player

1989   Named Most Valuable Player in Super Bowl XXIII; leads team in touchdowns and receptions

1990   Sets record of 3 receiving touchdowns in Super Bowl XXIV; leads NFL in receptions and receiving yardage; sets team records for one game production with 13 receptions, 5 touchdowns, and 30 points; sets team record for all-time yardage; named NFL Player of the Year by *Sports Illustrated*

1991   Leads team in receptions, yards, and touchdowns

1992   Becomes NFL all-time receiver of touchdown passes; sets team record of 106 consecutive games with at least 1 reception; leads team in receptions, yards gained.

STATISTICS

JERRY RICE
San Francisco 49ers

YEAR	G	RCPS	YDS	AVG	TDS
1985	16	49	927	18.9	3
1986	16	86	**1570**	18.3	16
1987	12	65	1078	16.6	**23**
1988	16	64	1306	20.4	10
1989	16	82	**1483**	18.1	**17**
1990	16	**100**	**1502**	15.0	13
1991	16	80	1206	15.1	14
1992	16	84	1201	14.3	11
1993	16	98	1503	15.3	15
TOTALS	140	708	11776	16.6	122

G	games
RCPS	receptions
YDS	yards
AVG	average
TDS	touchdowns

Bold indicates league-leading statistics

---

records held:

most receiving touchdowns, season: 22
most receiving touchdowns, career: 116
most postseason receptions, career: 75
most postseason touchdown receptions, career: 13
most consecutive games catching at least one touchdown: 13
most receiving yards, one Super Bowl game: 215
most touchdowns, one Super Bowl game: 3

SUGGESTIONS FOR FURTHER READING

Aaseng, Nathan. *College Football's Hottest Rivalries.* Minneapolis: Lerner, 1987.

Benagh, Jim. *Football: Startling Stories Behind the Records.* New York: Sterling Publishers, 1987.

Brenner, Richard J. *The Complete Super Bowl Story: Games I-XXIII.* Minneapolis: Lerner, 1990.

Duden, Jane, and Susan Osberg. *Football.* New York: Macmillan Publishing, 1991.

Rothaus, James R. *San Francisco Forty Niners.* Mankato, Minnesota: Creative Editions.

ABOUT THE AUTHORS

Rose Blue and Corinne J. Naden have each written well over a dozen young adult and children's books. Together they have written biographies of Barbara Bush, Whoopi Goldberg, Barbara Jordan, Christa McAuliffe, Ron McNair, and Colin Powell.

INDEX

PICTURE CREDITS
UPI/Bettmann Newsphotos: pp. 2, 8, 28, 37, 43, 48, 50, 54; AP/Wide World Photos: pp. 11, 26, 31, 34, 38, 58; Courtesy Greenwood Commonwealth, Greenwood, MI: pp. 16, 20, 21, 23; Reuters/Bettmann: pp. 44, 46, 53; courtesy San Francisco 49ers: pp. 40, 57.